In memory of Johnathon

Published by B&H Publishing Group

One Lifeway Plaza

Nashville, TN 37234-0164, USA

Dewey Decimal Classification: C242.5

SUBHD: DEVOTIONAL LITERATURE \ FAITH \ LOVE

Printed in Guangdong District, RRD Shenzhen, China, July 2016

1 2 3 4 5 6 20 19 18 17 16

Faith, Hope, Love
Devotional

100 Devotions for Kids and Parents to Share

by
Amy Parker

illustrations by Breezy Brookshire

B&H KIDS

Nashville, Tennessee

Contents

Faith

Faith Is . . .

Now faith is . . .
the proof of what is not seen.
—*Hebrews 11:1*

Faith. It's a word you may hear a lot. It may even be a word you use a lot.

"I have faith in you."

"Take a leap of faith!"

"A dog is a faithful friend."

But have you ever really tried to tell someone what it means? Hmm. That's a tough one. And when the going gets tough, the tough open their Bibles.

Hebrews 11 describes faith as "the proof of what is not seen." Like feeling the unseen wind on your face, faith is a feeling in your heart that just *knows*. God has told us about Himself, and we can trust what He has said. You *know* God created the universe. You *believe* He is always with you. God has no limits and is always everywhere. You *trust* that He is always listening. He is in control of everything. That knowing, that believing, that trusting is faith.

It grows over time with every little whisper from God. Every rainbow, every kiss on the forehead, and every answered prayer are all proof of God and the promises that He has for us.

Believe, trust, know . . . and your faith will continue to grow.

 Tell me about it:
In your own words, what is faith?

 Think about it:
What are some ways that God has whispered His love to you? How do you know He's there?

 DO IT!
Go out—today—and tell someone what *faith* means to you!

Seeing the Invisible

By faith we understand that the universe was created by God's command, so that what is seen has been made from things that are not visible.

—*Hebrews 11:3*

The very first sentence of the Bible says, "In the beginning God created the heavens and the earth" (Genesis 1:1). And that beginning is a perfect place to start building our faith.

When your faith feels weak and you wish you could actually see God, you can look around and *know*. Know that these amazing things that you can see and smell and touch—like mountains and monkeys and maple trees—came from "things that are not visible." The entire world came to be when your almighty Creator, your Savior, your God simply spoke.

When you start there, when you look around and know that the very first sentence in the Bible is true, it reminds you that the rest of His Word is too. When you read about God and His creation and His people, you *know*, you *believe*, you *feel* that it's real.

That, my friend, is faith. And see? Yours is already beginning to grow.

 Tell me about it:

What is one thing God created that completely amazes you?

 Think about it:

Now, go back to creation, and imagine that one thing being made. Can you picture God creating it out of nothing?

 DO IT!

Spend some time learning all you can about that one thing, and be amazed by what God can create by simply speaking a word.

Not by Sight

For we walk by faith, not by sight.

—*2 Corinthians 5:7*

We *can* look out at all that God created and know that He is there. But true faith is believing even though you can't see. As we spend time with God and grow closer to Him, we will have all the proof we need. (Remember Hebrews 11:1?)

Thomas, a disciple of Jesus, knew that Jesus had died on the cross. But when Thomas heard that Jesus was alive again, he said, "If I don't see the mark of the nails in His hands, . . . I will never believe!" (John 20:25). And who could blame him? It was quite a story!

Then Jesus Himself went to Thomas and showed him the marks in His hands. And Thomas believed. Jesus told Thomas, "Because you have seen Me, you have believed. Those who believe without seeing are blessed" (John 20:29).

Jesus *can* prove Himself to you. But let's be blessed by believing without seeing!

 Tell me about it:

What is one thing about Jesus that you think is hard to believe?

Think about it:

Think about all the things you know about God that are true. Why is this one thing different?

 DO IT!

Talk to God now and ask Him to help you believe without seeing.

13

Noah's Faith

By faith Noah, after he was warned about what was not yet seen and motivated by godly fear, built an ark to deliver his family.

—*Hebrews 11:7*

After Hebrews 11 explains faith, it gives us a lot of examples of faith heroes in the Bible. And Noah was definitely one of them.

Talk about believing in the unseen! God told Noah to build a huge boat with supplies he didn't have for a flood that wouldn't happen for years and years. And Noah listened!

God gave him exact details: "Use cypress wood. Build it this tall, this wide, and this high. Put the door here. Coat it with tar." And Noah obeyed every word.

In a world full of evil people who have turned away from God, Noah believed. Noah obeyed. Noah had faith. And as a result, his entire family was saved.

Tell me about it:
What are some ways that you obey God?

_____

_____

Think about it:
How could you be more like Noah in your obedience and faith?

_____

_____

DO IT!
Read (or ask someone to read to you) the whole story of Noah in Genesis 6–9.

Abraham's Faith

By faith he stayed as a foreigner in the land of promise . . . For he was looking forward to the city that has foundations, whose architect and builder is God.

—*Hebrews 11:9–10*

Do you ever wonder when God's promises are going to come true for *you*? I'm sure Abraham wondered the same thing.

God had promised to make Abraham "into a great nation" (Genesis 12:2), but Abraham spent much of his life living in a tent. God had promised Abraham that he would be the father of many people, as many as the stars in the sky (15:5). But at that moment, Abraham was the father of *no one*.

Still, Abraham held tight to the promises of God and followed where He led. Abraham knew that God would make His promises come true, no matter how difficult they seemed. And you know what? That's exactly what happened. Through Abraham, the Israelites (God's chosen people) became a great nation with as many people as the stars in the sky.

It can be hard to keep the faith when you don't see God's promises shining all around you. But hang in there. Keep following Him and holding tight to His promises. They will always be true.

 Tell me about it:

What are some promises that God has made to you? (See Deuteronomy 4:29; Philippians 4:19; Jeremiah 29:11; or 1 John 1:9 for starters.)

 Think about it:

If God can create a great nation out of Abraham, imagine what He can do with you!

 DO IT!

On the next clear night, try to count the stars in the sky just as God asked Abraham to do.

The Israelites' Faith

By faith [the Israelites] crossed the Red Sea as though they were on dry land.

—*Hebrews 11:29*

The Israelites had just left the only home they'd ever known. They were carrying everything they owned on their backs, pushing carts, pulling sheep. It was a loud, confusing mass of people and animals and stuff. But God's promise to set them free, to make them a great nation, was coming true. They were leaving the harsh rule of the Egyptians, headed to the home God had promised them.

Suddenly, the crowd halted. They had reached the edge of the Red Sea and could go no farther. But behind them, the Egyptian soldiers were coming. Fast. And they were *not* happy. Fear erupted in the crowd. But Moses looked to the Lord.

As Moses stretched his hand out over the sea, God sent a powerful wind that split the water in two, leaving a dry path for His people to walk through.

Would they make it safely across? And where was *across* anyway? They didn't know, but they knew that God was leading the way. So one by one, the people walked by faith through the middle of the Red Sea and into God's promises for them.

 Tell me about it:

Name a time when God has brought you safely through something that scared you.

 Think about it:

Imagine standing there, on a dry path in the middle of the Red Sea. What would you see, smell, feel?

 DO IT!

Take a moment to thank God for His constant protection, wherever He may lead.

Pleasing to God

Now without faith it is impossible to please God.

—*Hebrews 11:6*

Noah. Abraham. The Israelites. These faith heroes all had big roles in God's perfect plan.

But what would have happened if Noah hadn't built that boat?

Or if Abraham had given up on God's promise?

Or if the Israelites had never crossed that Red Sea?

We can't know for sure. But we do know this: because of their great faith, Noah, Abraham, and the Israelites pleased God and were able to play a big part in His plan.

Without faith, it's impossible. But *with faith*, well, you just never know where you may go.

 Tell me about it:

How did Noah, Abraham, and the Israelites please God?

 Think about it:

How can you play a part in God's plan?

 DO IT!

Do one thing today to step out in big faith!

Rewarding to Us

The one who draws near to Him must believe that He exists and rewards those who seek Him.

—*Hebrews 11:6*

Just as our faith pleases God, it can also bring big rewards. No, you probably won't get a trophy or even an ice cream cone. God's rewards are actually much bigger than that.

You may find His rewards in the warmth of a sunshiny day or the smile of a friend. But we could never count or measure the rewards given to those who seek, learn about, and become closer to God throughout their lives. The lasting reward of a faith-filled life stretches all the way into eternity.

A life of seeking (looking for) God will not always be easy. But it will always be the most rewarding way to live—both here on earth and in heaven.

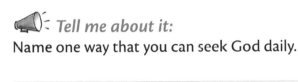 *Tell me about it:*

Name one way that you can seek God daily.

 Think about it:

How did God reward Noah, Abraham, or the Israelites for their faithfulness?

 DO IT!

Create a medal for yourself with the words "Seek Him," to always remind you of the life God rewards.

Faith Is Strong

By faith the walls of Jericho fell down after being encircled by the Israelites for seven days.

—*Hebrews 11:30*

Even for the faithful, sometimes God's plans seem plain silly. Just ask Joshua.

When Moses died, God chose Joshua to lead the Israelites into their promised land. The first stop was Jericho, a big city that God had given to the Israelites. But there was only one problem: there was a humongous wall around Jericho.

So God told Joshua how to get in. "Look, I've already given the city to you. March around the city one time for six days. Then on the seventh day, go around seven times, have the priests blow the trumpets, and tell the people to shout. Then the wall will fall" (see Joshua 6:1–5).

Wait . . . *what?* No bulldozers? No battering rams?

Nope. Just faith in the mighty hand of God.

And you know what? The Israelites marched—one round for six days, seven rounds on the seventh. Then, when those trumpets blasted and the people shouted, the walls came crumbling down.

Hmm. So maybe we should follow God's instructions, whether they make sense to us or not. And when we do, the walls just may fall, clearing the way to all of God's promises for us.

 Tell me about it:

How did Joshua react to God's directions?

 Think about it:

What are some directions God gives you?

 DO IT!

Spend your day trying to listen to and follow God's directions to you. Then tomorrow, try it again! And the next day, and the next . . .

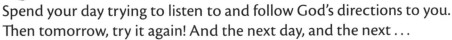

Find the Faithful

And what more can I say?
Time is too short for me to
tell about Gideon, Barak,
Samson, Jephthah, David,
Samuel, and the prophets.

—*Hebrews 11:32*

By Hebrews 11:32, the writer's hand must have been getting tired. "What more can I say?" he asked. He had told us about the faith of Abel and Enoch and Noah and Abraham and Sarah and Isaac and Jacob and didn't have time for Gideon, Barak, Samson, Jephthah, David . . . Whew! Now *my* hand is getting tired!

There are so many examples of obedient, faithful people in the Bible. There are so many heroes to look up to and to guide us when we need help. But you know what? Those people are all around us too. Our parents and teachers and maybe even that big brother can help guide us through this walk with God.

So when your faith needs a boost, look to those faithful people around you for support. And remember Abel and Enoch and Noah and Abraham and . . . well, you get the picture. God has surrounded us with all we need in this walk of faith; we'll never have to walk alone.

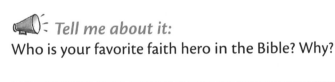 *Tell me about it:*

Who is your favorite faith hero in the Bible? Why?

_____

_____

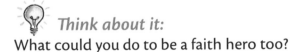 *Think about it:*

What could you do to be a faith hero too?

_____

_____

 DO IT!

Know someone else who could use a faith boost? Give him or her one today!

Faithful Steps

He guards the steps of His faithful ones.
—*1 Samuel 2:9*

All of those faithful Bible heroes and all of the faithful people around you—they all have one thing in common. God guards their steps. And He will do the same for you.

Don't you love the way 1 Samuel 2:9 says, "His faithful ones"? Those who are *His* are faithful. He calls us His own. We are precious treasures of the Creator of the universe. And He guards our every step.

When you're a little afraid of where God is leading, when you're feeling unsure about that next step, remember to be faithful. He has promised to protect you, guarding each step as you go.

 *Tell me about it:*

Name one person from the Bible whom God protected. How did He protect him or her?

_____

_____

 Think about it:

How does God protect you?

_____

_____

DO IT!

Trace the outline of your foot, and write 1 Samuel 2:9 on it. Keep it as a reminder that God guards your steps.

Above All

Above all, fear the LORD and worship
Him faithfully with all your heart.
—*1 Samuel 12:24*

What do you love more than anything? Baseball? Bubble gum? Barbie dolls?

Okay, okay, that's kind of a trick question. First Samuel 12:24 tells us that "above all" we should worship God faithfully. To be honest, few of us could say that we truly put God first. We get caught up in school and games and friends, and we sometimes forget that the Creator of the universe is watching over us and waiting to hear from us.

I get it. It's hard to put something first when we don't see it in front of us all the time. And it's hard to worship someone we don't know a whole lot about, right? That's why it's so important to spend time with God every day, to get to know Him, to talk to Him, to read His Word. And the more you learn about Him, the more you hear from Him, the more you'll *want* to worship Him and put Him absolutely first.

After all, He created us. He gave His only Son for us. Placing Him "above all" is the very least we can do.

 Tell me about it:

It's okay. Be honest. Right now, what do you put first?

 Think about it:

Why should God come absolutely first?

 DO IT!

What is *one* way you could put God first today? Do it.
Today and every day.

Friends of Faith

Then Saul's son Jonathan came to David in Horesh and encouraged him in his faith in God.

—*1 Samuel 23:16*

Do you have a friend who's always smiling . . . who tells you the favorite thing she learned at church that week . . . who treats others the way Jesus would? We all need friends to encourage us in our faith.

David and Jonathan were friends like that. The Bible says that Jonathan loved David "as much as he loved himself" (1 Samuel 18:1). And when David was running scared, in fear for his life, Jonathan found him and reminded him of God's promise to protect him. Jonathan's encouragement kept David going strong.

David and Jonathan were friends of faith, a friendship given and created by God. That is exactly the kind of friends we need. And that's exactly the kind of friend we each need to be.

 Tell me about it:

Name one friend who encourages you in your faith.

_____

_____

 Think about it:

How can you cheer others on as they learn more about God?

_____

_____

 DO IT!

Make cards with your favorite Bible verses on them. Give the cards to your friends to encourage their faith!

More Than Most

Then I put my brother Hanani in charge of Jerusalem . . . because he was a faithful man who feared God more than most.

—*Nehemiah 7:2*

When Nehemiah was looking for someone to take charge of the city of Jerusalem, he chose his brother. He didn't choose him because he was big or strong or handsome. He didn't even choose him because he was his brother. Nehemiah chose Hanani because "he was a faithful man."

When people look at you, do they see your faith? First Timothy 4:12 tells us that even young people "should be an example to the believers in speech, in conduct, in love, in faith, in purity." So always remember that the way you act, the way you talk, and the way you believe should be a good example to everyone—even the grown-ups.

 Tell me about it:

What are some words people might use to describe you?

_____

_____

 Think about it:

What are some ways you can show your faith?

_____

_____

 DO IT!

Write the letters of your name straight down in a column. Now use one word that starts with each of those letters to describe yourself. (Turn to the blank pages at the back of this book to find room for these "Do It!" activities and other thoughts!)

Set Apart

Know that the LORD has set apart the faithful for Himself.

—*Psalm 4:3*

Let's imagine that there are two lines. In the first line are the people God has set apart for Himself. In the second line is everybody else. Which line would *you* want to be in?

I don't know about you, but I'm picking the God line. Still, to be in that line, I've got to be faithful. I need to believe in God and His Word and be obedient to them both.

With the choices we make and the actions we take, we are choosing which line we want to stand in. Choose the line of faithful people, the ones set apart for God.

 Tell me about it:

What do you think it means to be "set apart" for God?

_____

_____

Think about it:

How can you choose to be one of the faithful?

_____

_____

DO IT!

Every time you make a decision today, stop and ask if it's the right choice, the one that sets you apart for God. Make the choices of the faithful, knowing that you are set apart for God.

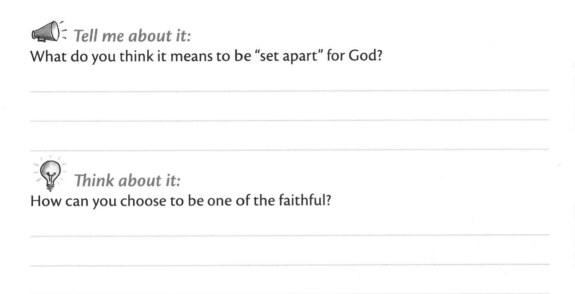

Love the Lord

Love the LORD, all His faithful ones.
—*Psalm 31:23*

How do you show love to your family? Do you spend time with them? Talk with them? Listen to them?

Psalm 31:23 reminds the faithful ones—you and me—to love the Lord too. How exactly can we show our love for the Lord? Well, we can spend time with Him, talk to Him, and listen to Him, like we do with our family. But Jesus tells us another way to show our love: "If you love Me, you will keep My commands" (John 14:15).

It can be hard to follow all of God's commands all the time, but God knows our hearts. He knows when we're trying to do what's right and keep His commands. And when we do, it's one way we can love the Lord.

Loving the Lord is just what we "faithful ones" do. Let's try to do it the way He asks us to.

 Tell me about it:
How does God show His love for you?

_____

_____

 Think about it:
Why do you think it's important that we show our love for Him?

_____

_____

 DO IT!
Sing a song. Say a prayer. Obey a command. Find some ways to show God how much you love Him today.

Never Alone

For the LORD loves justice and will not abandon His faithful ones.

—*Psalm 37:28*

No matter how much we love God, He will always love us more. One way He loves us is by always being with us. Psalm 37:28 tells us that God "will not abandon His faithful ones." He will never leave us alone.

Wherever we are and whatever we're doing, God is always there. He's always watching. He's always listening. And He's always loving us, His faithful ones. It's just one of the many ways He rewards the faithful. (Remember Hebrews 11:6?)

So when you feel afraid or lonely, remember that He is there. He will not leave you.

 Tell me about it:

Was there ever a time when you felt all alone? What happened?

_____

_____

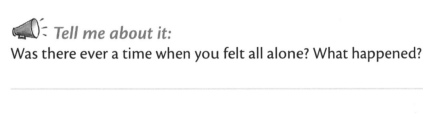 *Think about it:*

If you had known God was listening at that time, what would you have said to Him?

_____

_____

 DO IT!

Draw a picture of the time when you felt alone. Write the words of Psalm 37:28 across the bottom as a reminder that He is always there.

A Faithful Hero

The LORD is faithful in all His words and gracious in all His actions.
—*Psalm 145:13*

There's no way to get around it: people just aren't perfect. We mess up. We say mean things. And we hurt people's feelings.

Isn't it so nice to know that God is nothing like that? He *is* perfect. He doesn't mess up. And He doesn't make mistakes. He is "faithful" and "gracious in all His actions."

He will never lead us the wrong way. He will never go back on His Word. And He loves us more than we could ever imagine.

So when your heroes let you down, when the world seems scary and mean, put your faith in the one, true Hero: God. He will never let you down.

 Tell me about it:

Who are some of your heroes?

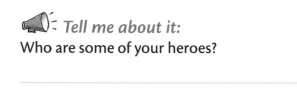

 Think about it:

Has a hero ever let you down? How did that make you feel?

 *DO IT!*

Draw a picture of your perfect superhero. And remember the Hero who is always by your side.

Written on Your Heart

Never let loyalty and faithfulness leave you. Tie them around your neck; write them on the tablet of your heart.
—*Proverbs 3:3*

Having faith everywhere you go, all the time, is tough.

People won't always agree with it. They won't always understand it. And they won't always support you in it.

The writer of Proverbs knew that. (And I'm pretty sure God knows that too.) That's why Proverbs 3:3 tells us to do whatever we've got to do to keep the faith. Tie it around your neck. Write it on your heart. Put it in your pocket. Print it on your T-shirt. But whatever you do, never, ever, ever let your faith leave you.

Faith takes work, but it's always worth it. Keep it close. You never know when you'll need it most.

Tell me about it:

Has anyone ever disagreed with your faith?

_____

_____

Think about it:

What are some things you can do when that happens?

_____

_____

DO IT!

Create a keepsake—a drawing, a Bible verse, or any little token—to remind you of your faith. Take it with you wherever you go.

God's Delight

Lying lips are detestable to the LORD,
but faithful people are His delight.

—*Proverbs 12:22*

Did you know that you're a delight to the Lord? Yes, you. Little ol' you.

Your faithfulness makes God happy. Your worship makes Him smile. When you love Him and serve Him and tell people about Him, you bring joy to the Creator of the universe.

So when you're feeling small, when you think nothing you do matters at all, remember that God sees you. He loves you. And He delights in your faithfulness.

 Tell me about it:

Name some ways that you have made God happy today.

_____

_____

 Think about it:

Why do you think our faithfulness makes Him happy?

_____

_____

 DO IT!

Draw a sad face and a happy face on a piece of paper. Under the sad face, list things that you think make God sad. Under the happy face, put things that make Him happy.

Blessed

A faithful man will have many blessings.
—*Proverbs 28:20*

We've learned a lot about being faithful so far. And by this point, Proverbs 28:20 is probably no surprise.

After all, we know that God is always with the faithful (Psalm 37:28). We know that our faithfulness makes God happy (Proverbs 12:22). And we know that God rewards those who try to find Him (Hebrews 11:6).

The message of Proverbs 28:20 is one the Bible shows us again and again. God wants us always to remember that He cares for the faithful. And although the faithful will face tough times, in the end, their lives will be blessed.

Knowing that this verse is true, how will you choose to live today and every day?

 Tell me about it:

How is the message of Proverbs 28:20 true in your own life?

_____

_____

_____

 *Think about it:*

Can you think of other people you know or people in the Bible whose lives were blessed because of their faithfulness?

_____

_____

_____

 DO IT!

Draw or make a list of your many blessings. Write Proverbs 28:20 at the top.

Stand Firm

"If you do not stand firm in your faith, then you will not stand at all."
—*Isaiah 7:9*

If you were building a big tower of blocks, would you build it on the floor? Or in a big bowl of Jell-O? Umm, the floor, right? Why? Because it's a firm foundation!

It's the same when you're building your life. You want to build it on something strong, steady, and everlasting—like a strong, steady, everlasting God. If you don't, Isaiah tells us, "you will not stand at all."

When you place your faith in stuff or even people, things can get wobbly. Stuff doesn't last very long, and people just aren't perfect. But when you place your faith in God, you know you've got a firm foundation to build a life on.

 Tell me about it:

What are some things, besides God, that you place your faith in?

_____

_____

Think about it:

Why is God the best foundation to build your life on?

_____

_____

DO IT!

Get out some blocks and try building towers in different places and on different foundations. Which works best? Why?

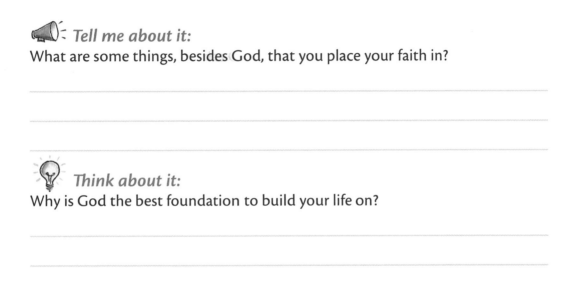

Live by Faith

The righteous one will live by his faith.
—*Habakkuk 2:4*

Sometimes the difference between right and wrong can get a bit fuzzy. Is it wrong to tell Mom that dinner was good—when it was really kind of gross? I'm not sure I can answer that. . . .

But the Bible does give us a lot of clear-cut answers about right and wrong. Just take a look at the Ten Commandments (Exodus 20:1–17). Or listen to Jesus talk about the greatest commandments (Mark 12:28–31). And one more answer is right here in Habakkuk: live by faith.

We've talked a lot about living by faith—how to do it and what it looks like in your life. And Habakkuk reminds us that every time you take a step of faith, it's a step in the right direction.

 Tell me about it:

In your own words, what does *righteous* mean? (Ask your parents if you need help!)

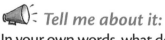 *Think about it:*

Why do you think God wants us to be righteous?

 DO IT!

Write the word *righteous* in the middle of a piece of paper. Now, in all different colors, write as many words as you can think of that describe a person who is righteous.

Fearless

But He said to them, "Why are you fearful, you of little faith?"
—*Matthew 8:26*

The disciples were getting the hang of this faith thing. They had walked with Jesus as He preached. They had seen the many miracles He performed.

But then came the storm.

Jesus and His disciples were all in a boat, crossing the Sea of Galilee, when the wind started whipping and the waves started crashing. All they could see were the flashes of lightning and the driving rain. They couldn't hear over the thunder and the wind. But they could feel the water rushing around their feet—and rising. Where was Jesus?!?

They found Him—sleeping peacefully—at the back of the boat. "Jesus!" the grown men cried. "We're all going to die!!!"

Jesus opened His eyes and answered with an unexpected question: "Why are you afraid, you of little faith?" Then He turned to the storm. "Shh. Be quiet. Be still." And the wind and the waves obeyed.

It's pretty easy to keep our faith when the sun is shining and all is well. But the true test of our faith is when the scary days come. That's when we need to remember that Jesus is in control. He can even calm the storms.

 Tell me about it:

When is the last time something scary or stormy happened in your life?

 Think about it:

Would Jesus have said you had big faith or little faith during that time?

 DO IT!

On a piece of paper, draw the stormy scene from above. Then write the words from Matthew 8:27: "Even the winds and the sea obey Him!"

Faith You Can See

Seeing their faith, Jesus told
the paralytic, "Have courage, son,
your sins are forgiven."

—*Matthew 9:2*

Not everyone had "little faith" like the disciples in the storm. Sometimes people would step up and show Jesus big faith.

One man had heard of Jesus' healing power, but he couldn't go to see Him because he was paralyzed. Day and night, the man just lay there on a mat on the ground. But when the man's friends heard that Jesus was coming to town, they picked up the man—mat and all—and carried him to see Jesus.

When Jesus saw their great faith, He told the paralyzed man, "Get up, pick up your mat, and go home" (Matthew 9:6). Because this man and his friends had stepped out in big faith, Jesus quickly healed him and sent him on his way.

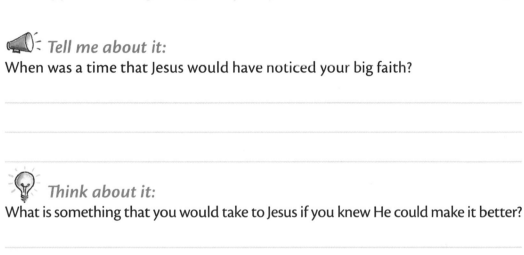

Tell me about it:

When was a time that Jesus would have noticed your big faith?

_____

_____

Think about it:

What is something that you would take to Jesus if you knew He could make it better?

_____

_____

 DO IT!

What is that one thing that you need to have big faith about? Take it to Jesus right now, and trust Him to take care of you.

"Why Did You Doubt?"

Immediately Jesus reached out His hand, caught hold of him, and said to him, "You of little faith, why did you doubt?"
—*Matthew 14:31*

The disciples were out on the water again when they saw a figure walking toward them on the sea. "It's a ghost!" they cried. But the voice answered, "Don't be afraid. It's Me, Jesus."

"Lord, if it's You," Peter tested, "let me walk to You on the water."

"Okay, come," the voice answered.

So Peter, in big faith, climbed out of the boat. And to everyone's surprise, he started walking out to Jesus on the sea! But then Peter noticed the howling wind. It scared him, and he began to sink. "Save me!" he cried to Jesus. And the steady hand of Jesus pulled Peter up.

Peter had stepped out in big faith. Then he lost it when things got scary. But you know the best part? Jesus was there to catch Peter, even when he lost his faith. And Jesus will catch you too.

 Tell me about it:

Was there ever a time when you got scared and were filled with doubt?

_____

_____

_____

 Think about it:

Did you call to Jesus for help? What happened?

_____

_____

_____

 DO IT!

Fill a bowl with water. Try placing different items (like a paper clip, a penny, a leaf) on top of the water to see if they float.

Mustard-Seed Faith

"I assure you: If you have faith the size of a mustard seed, you will tell this mountain, 'Move from here to there,' and it will move. Nothing will be impossible for you."
—*Matthew 17:20*

Do you know how tiny a mustard seed is? It's a lot smaller than a watermelon seed or a sunflower seed. If you held one, it would just be a little dot in the middle of your hand.

But Jesus tells us that this is all we need—faith that big, the size of a mustard seed.

Do you ever feel like you have mountains to move? Do you have problems so big that you don't know how you'll get around them? Or do you have dreams so huge that you don't know how you'll ever reach them?

You just need a little faith. Tiny faith, even. Jesus said even with that, "Nothing will be impossible for you."

 *Tell me about it:*

What is one problem you need help with?

 Think about it:

What do you dream of doing one day?

 DO IT!

Talk to Jesus right now about both of those things. And have a little mustard-seed faith that He will help you with your problems, your dreams, and everything in between.

Faithful over a Few

"You were faithful over a few things; I will put you in charge of many things."
—Matthew 25:23

When you brush your teeth, are you careful to clean every one? Or do you quickly run the toothbrush under the water without ever touching your teeth? When you clean your room, do you put everything neatly in its place? Or kick everything under the bed?

We can tell ourselves that these little things don't matter. We may try to skimp on the things that we think no one will notice. But Jesus tells us in Matthew that these things matter too. And they don't just matter; they prepare us for bigger things. If we do a good job on the little things, we'll get even bigger things to be in charge of.

Even if there were no reward, no bigger prizes waiting, we should work in a way that would make God proud. "In all the work you are doing, work the best you can. Work as if you were doing it for the Lord" (Colossians 3:23 NCV). And when we do, when we are faithful with the little things, big things will come our way.

 Tell me about it:

What is one little job that you don't like doing?

_____

_____

 Think about it:

Do you try your best on that job? Why or why not?

_____

_____

_____

 DO IT!

Make a list of chores to do around the house. At the bottom, in colorful letters, write the words of Colossians 3:23.

Grow Our Faith

The apostles said to the Lord,
"Increase our faith."
—*Luke 17:5*

When being faithful with the little things is hard . . . when you don't even have a speck-of-dirt-size faith . . . where do you go? What do you do?

Well, the disciples went to Jesus, and they just asked, "Lord, increase our faith." They had seen Him heal the sick, help blind men to see, and feed thousands of people with a little boy's lunch. But they were still having trouble. As much as their faith had grown, they still needed more.

"Increase our faith." Make it grow. And you know what? I believe Jesus did just that.

He's been here on this earth, He knows it's tough, and He's here to help.

All we have to do is ask.

 Tell me about it:

When has your faith been the strongest?

 Think about it:

When was a time that your faith was weak?

 DO IT!

Ask Jesus now to grow your faith. And just by knowing He will, your faith will already begin to grow.

Forgiveness by Faith

"By faith in Me they may receive forgiveness of sins."
—*Acts 26:18*

Maybe the best, most important part of our faith comes down to this: forgiveness.

John 3:16 tells us about God's perfect plan to forgive us: "For God loved the world in this way: He gave His One and Only Son, so that everyone who believes in Him will not perish but have eternal life."

Everybody messes up. None of us can be perfect. But Jesus, God's Son and the only perfect person to ever walk the earth, took all of our sins for us. When we believe in Him and ask Him to forgive us, He does. And our sins no longer get in the way of our relationship with a holy God. We can be close to Him, talk to Him, and know Him.

All of this is possible with faith. Our sins can be forgiven by a holy God who loves us so much that He gave the life of His only Son to make ours better.

 Tell me about it:

Why does God care if we sin?

_____

_____

 Think about it:

How does Jesus make forgiveness possible?

_____

_____

DO IT!

Talk to God about your sins and your need for forgiveness. And thank Him for making a way for us to have forgiveness through faith.

Stand by Faith

They were broken off by unbelief,
but you stand by faith.

—*Romans 11:20*

Today's verse is only once sentence, but it says so much about faith. There's a clear difference in the two groups of people: *they* and *you*.

They didn't believe. They were broken off. *You* have faith. You stand strong.

As complicated as faith may seem sometimes, it really can be this simple. Do you have faith or don't you? Do you believe or do you not? Are you a *you* or are you a *they*?

The good news is: no one is beyond God's reach. God will add the *theys* to the *yous* if they choose to believe.

And together we can all stand strong in faith.

 Tell me about it:

Why do you choose to believe?

 Think about it:

Think of someone who may not believe yet. How could you help him or her see why you believe?

 DO IT!

Make a card, sing a song, or draw a picture for someone who does not believe yet. Ask God to show you how you can help him find his way to believe.

Victory!

This is the victory that has
conquered the world: our faith.
—1 John 5:4

Faith can be a tough concept to grasp. We can't see it. We can't touch it. And we don't always understand it.

But I love the way it is described in 1 John 5:4. It's so real, so powerful; you can almost see it.

In the end, faith wins. Our God and our faith in Him are ultimately victorious over all the evil in this world. And to me, that makes it all worth it.

Stand strong in your faith. It truly will conquer the world.

 Tell me about it:

How can faith conquer anything, especially the world?

 Think about it:

What are some ways—today and every day—that you can fight the bad of this world with your faith?

 DO IT!

What does our world look like when it is conquered by faith? Draw a picture or write a short story about it.

Faith and Hope

Now faith is the reality of what is hoped for.
—*Hebrews 11:1*

For more than thirty days now, we've learned about faith, talked about faith, and grown in faith. And next we're going to move on to *hope*.

Faith and hope go hand in hand. Faith is knowing that everything we hope for is real. Faith is knowing that hope isn't just a bubble that will pop and disappear. Faith is knowing that hope will come true—so true, you can hold it in your hands.

Faith and *hope* may be difficult for us to take hold of, but the Bible tells us that these things—faith, hope, and love—are the three things that last forever (1 Corinthians 13:13). And since they'll be around forever, well, we might as well get to know them better.

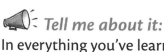 *Tell me about it:*

In everything you've learned about faith so far, what is the one thing you remember the most?

 Think about it:

How do faith and hope work together?

 DO IT!

On a piece of paper, in big letters, write your favorite verse about faith. Decorate it, draw a border around it, color it, and hang it where you will see it every day.

Hope

Have Hope

You should have confidence because you respect God; you should have hope because you are innocent.

—*Job 4:6* NCV

Have you heard the story of Job? If so, you may be thinking it has little to do with *hope*. Even though God Himself described Job as "an honest and innocent man" (Job 1:1 NCV), Job lost everything: his children, his wealth, and his health.

Pretty hopeless, huh?

But when you look closer, you see the word *hope* all over the book of Job—eighteen times, in fact—more than almost every other book of the Bible. Job's story is the ultimate test of hope, and he passed with flying colors. No matter what Satan threw at him, Job refused to blame God. Even though Job didn't understand why it was happening, his hope in God remained.

In the end, God gave Job ten more children and *doubled* the riches he had lost. God rewarded Job for having hope in Him. And He will do the same for you.

 *Tell me about it:*

Describe a time that felt hopeless to you.

 Think about it:

How did it turn out? Was it really, truly "hopeless"?

 DO IT!

Read the last chapter of Job's story, Job 42, and know that God wants to be your source of hope too.

The Hope Factory

Patience produces character,
and character produces hope.

—*Romans 5:4 NCV*

What if we could have our own little hope factory? You know, a way to produce hope whenever we need it, creating it in an endless supply.

Well, Romans 5:4 tells us exactly how to do that.

First, you take a little patience. Or maybe a whole lot of patience—depending on how much hope you want to make. You patiently wait for God's answers. You patiently watch for His plans. You patiently listen for His will. And before you know it, a little *character* rolls off the factory line.

Then you mold that character into shape. You make good decisions. You think better thoughts. You have better behavior. And that's when you start to see your final product: hope.

The more you work at this process, the more you know this process works. And that produces hope for better things. So, when you get discouraged, just keep piling on the patience; then character will grow and rise into hope.

 Tell me about it:

Are you needing a little extra hope? Why?

Think about it:

What could you do if you had an endless supply of hope?

DO IT!

On a piece of paper, draw your hope factory.

Strength and Courage

Be strong and courageous, all you who
put your hope in the LORD.
—*Psalm 31:24*

What are you afraid of? Thunderstorms? Math tests? The big dog next door?

Well, you don't have to be afraid. There may be a lot of scary things in this world, but God is bigger than all those things. And when you put your hope and faith and trust in Him, He becomes a part of you. He lives inside you. And "the One who is in you is greater than the one who is in the world" (1 John 4:4).

When you put your hope in God, you become braver. You become stronger. And everything else becomes a lot less scary.

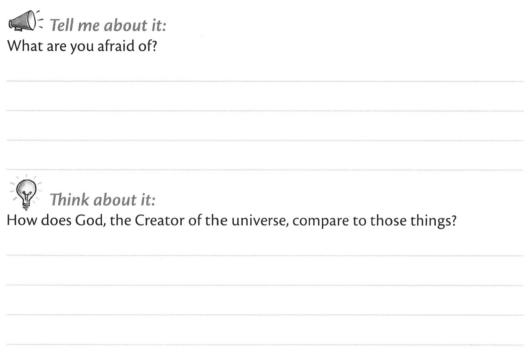

Tell me about it:
What are you afraid of?

_____

_____

_____

Think about it:
How does God, the Creator of the universe, compare to those things?

_____

_____

_____

DO IT!
Talk to God for a minute. Tell Him that you put your hope in Him, and ask Him to give you the strength and courage to face the things that scare you.

Faithful Love

May Your faithful love rest on us,
Yahweh, for we put our hope in You.
—*Psalm 33:22*

What do you put your hope in? Who do you trust with your future? What do you depend on to make your dreams come true? Your parents? Your friends? Your toys? Your home?

All of those are good things, but there's one place we can put our hope that will never let us down. And that is *in the Lord.*

Our parents can't always be there to guide us. Our friends, our toys, even our homes will come and go. But God lasts forever. He knows and sees everything. You can't even imagine His love for you, and His love lasts forever (Psalm 136:1).

Put your hope in the Lord, and His "faithful love" will never let you down.

 *Tell me about it:*

Tell about a time when someone let you down.

 Think about it:

Can you remember a time when you let someone else down?

 DO IT!

Make sure you forgive the person who let you down, and ask forgiveness (if you haven't already) for letting someone else down. And remember to put your hope in God, who will never let us down.

He Will Answer

I put my hope in You, LORD;
You will answer, Lord my God.

—*Psalm 38:15*

When you read today's verse, what do you think? Do you *really* believe it's true?

When you pray, when you tell God your worries, when you ask for God's help, do you really expect Him to answer?

He *will*, you know. You may not hear it, and it may not be right away. But over time, you will see it. You will *feel* it.

So as you pray today, say it like you mean it. Say it like God is listening. Say it as if He will answer you.

Because *He will.*

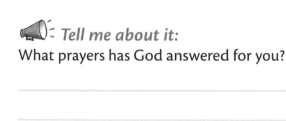 *Tell me about it:*

What prayers has God answered for you?

 Think about it:

What is a prayer that God *hasn't* answered? Why do you think that is?

 DO IT!

Get a small notebook or a piece of paper. Start a list of prayers that God has answered. As that list grows, your hope in the Lord will grow too.

What Are You Waiting For?

Now, Lord, what do I wait for?
My hope is in You.

—*Psalm 39:7*

Now that your hope is in the Lord . . . Now that your strength comes from Him . . . Now that you have nothing to fear . . .

What are you waiting for?!

What is that big, crazy dream? Or that tiny thing you wanted to change? Or that person you want to become friends with?

You can do it! All of it! Your hopes, your dreams, are waiting! Your fears and worries are gone!

Only hope in Him, and take the next step.

Come on! What are you waiting for?

 *Tell me about it:*

What's one thing you've always wanted to do?

 Think about it:

Why haven't you done it?

 DO IT!

Today, think of that one thing you want to do, something you know God is guiding you to do, and DO IT.

The Cure for Sadness

Why am I so sad? Why am I so upset?
I should put my hope in God and
keep praising him.

—*Psalm 42:5 NCV*

There are a lot of sad things that can happen in life. Friends may move away. You may get sick or hurt. You may lose a pet or a loved one.

We can't know for sure why sad things happen to us. They may help us learn and grow. They can help us enjoy the happy times even more.

But there's one thing we know for sure: even when bad things happen, when we feel sad and out of control, God still loves us. And He is still in control.

So when sad days come, as hard as it may seem, remember to put your hope in God, and "keep praising Him."

Tell me about it:
When is the last time you were really sad?

_____

_____

Think about it:
Did you know that, even then, God was watching over you, loving you?

_____

_____

DO IT!
On a piece of paper, write Psalm 42:5 in bright, colorful letters. Then the next time you're sad, remember to put your hope in God.

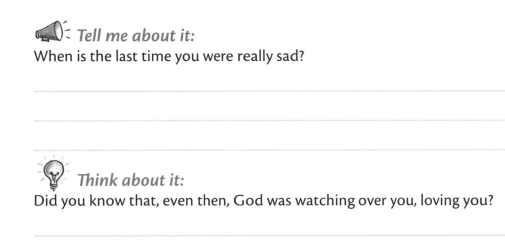

What He Has Done

I will praise You forever for what You
have done . . . I will put my hope in
Your name, for it is good.

—*Psalm 52:9*

Have you ever been told to "count your blessings"? Have you ever done it? Do you know what it means?

Counting your blessings is simply remembering, listing, *counting* all of the wonderful things God has done for you. When we do, as Psalm 52:9 tells us, we remember to praise God for those things. We remember why we put our hope in Him.

So when your hope is weak, when it seems like there's little to hope for, take a look back at all the things He has done in your life. Count your blessings. Thank Him. And remember that there's a whole list of good reasons why you put your hope in Him.

 Tell me about it:

Does your hope get weak? When?

 Think about it:

How can counting your blessings help make your hope stronger?

 DO IT!

Let's do it now: count your blessings. Make a list of all the ways God has blessed you. And when your hope starts to dim, get out your list and count them again.

Awe-Inspiring Works

You answer us in righteousness, with awe-inspiring works, God of our salvation, the hope of all the ends of the earth and of the distant seas.

—*Psalm 65:5*

Take a moment—right now—to look at the world around you. You won't have to look very far to find something awesome.

The flowers of spring. The sunset on the horizon. The fiery colors of fall. The stars in the sky. God personally crafted, handmade, built from scratch every single one of these awe-inspiring things—and so much more.

This is the God who created you. *This* is the God watching over you. *This* is the God you can put your hope in.

Always remember that the God of these "awe-inspiring works" is the very God who holds your hand.

 Tell me about it:

What do you think is the most awesome thing God created?

 Think about it:

Imagine being there as God created that one thing. Listen to Him speak. See it taking shape. How awesome is our God!

 DO IT!

Draw a picture of one of God's awe-inspiring works. Share it with someone you love.

False Hope

Place no trust in oppression, or false hope in robbery. If wealth increases, pay no attention to it.

—*Psalm 62:10*

You wouldn't go rock climbing with a paper chain for a rope. You wouldn't explore a cave with a candle for a light. And you wouldn't go camping with a box for a tent. Well . . . I guess you *could*, but it probably wouldn't end well.

It's just the same with life. You have to be very careful where you place your hope. When you place your hope in the wrong places, it only sets you up to be disappointed or even hurt.

When you go rock climbing, you choose the strongest rope. When you explore a cave, you shine a flashlight that won't burn out. When you go camping, you sleep in a weatherproof tent.

And when you need someone to lean on *for life*, you don't pick a false hope. You put your hope in God.

 *Tell me about it:*

Where are some places where you place your hope?

_____

_____

_____

 Think about it:

How have those things supported you? How have they let you down?

_____

_____

_____

 DO IT!

Make a list of everything you'd need for your survival kit for life.

Rest in Him

Rest in God alone, my soul,
for my hope comes from Him.
—*Psalm 62:5*

Think about your snuggliest blanket, your softest pillow, the coziest spot in the house. Imagine you're in that spot, lying on the pillow, wrapped in that blanket. Maybe even a plate of warm chocolate chip cookies is waiting nearby. Rest doesn't get any better than that, does it?

Yes. Yes, it does.

Not only can you have your blanket, your pillow, your cozy spot—and even your cookies!—you can rest in God, the Creator of the entire universe.

There is nothing you will face that He cannot handle. Just place all of your worries, your fears, your hopes, and your dreams in His hands. And rest in Him.

 *Tell me about it:*

Where's your favorite place to snuggle up for a nap?

_____

_____

 Think about it:

What does it mean to rest in God?

_____

_____

 DO IT!

Draw a great big hand on a piece of paper. Then write any worries, fears, hopes, and dreams on that hand. Imagine yourself giving all of it to God for Him to take care of. Now rest in Him.

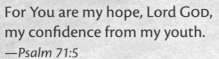

My Hope, My Confidence

For You are my hope, Lord GOD,
my confidence from my youth.
—*Psalm 71:5*

Do you ever wonder ... *Am I good enough for the team? Am I smart enough to keep up? Why would she want to be my friend?*

Well, stop wondering. Stop worrying. And put your confidence in God. He answers with ... "You are my child" (1 John 3:1). "You are my creation" (Ephesians 2:10). "And you are wonderfully made" (Psalm 139:14).

Whenever you begin to doubt yourself, remember what God says about you. Let your confidence be *in Him*.

 Tell me about it:

When do you doubt yourself?

_____

_____

 Think about it:

What would God say about your doubts?

_____

_____

 DO IT!

Make a list of the doubts you've had about yourself. Now, beside each doubt, write what God says about you.

Day and Night

I rise before dawn and cry out for help; I put my hope in Your word. I am awake through each watch of the night to meditate on Your promise.

—*Psalm 119:147–148*

When do you talk to God? In the mornings? At bedtime? Before meals?

Our hope will grow stronger with every moment that we think about or "meditate on" God and His promises. And we will learn more about God and those promises every time we read His Word.

Reading devotionals (like this one!) is a great start. But are there other ways you could be spending more time with Him? Starting each day with a prayer? Reading your Bible every night?

God will reward every moment—day and night—that you spend talking to Him, thinking about Him, and learning about Him and His Word. Not only will you grow closer to the One who knows you best; you will gain hope through His promises for you.

 Tell me about it:

How often do you spend time with God?

_____

_____

_____

 Think about it:

Could you spend more time with God? How would that help you?

_____

_____

_____

DO IT!

Make a simple schedule of the time you want to spend with God.

God's Promises = Hope

Remember Your word to Your servant;
You have given me hope through it.

—*Psalm 119:49*

The Bible is full of God's promises to His people. You can see His promise to Noah—and to us—with a vibrant rainbow resting in the clouds. You can hear His promise to make Abraham's family have as many people as the stars in the sky—and see it unfold before your very eyes. You'll hear God promise to rescue His people from a mean pharaoh—and watch the Israelites march to safety through the middle of the Red Sea. And best of all, you'll read of His promises to send a Savior to the world—and then hear the angels rejoice as that baby, God's Son, is born to us in Bethlehem.

These promises were written just for us, to give us hope, to remind us of God's great love for His people—for *you* and for me. Take time to read those promises, because when all else fails, God's promises will always be true.

 Tell me about it:
Why do you think God wants us to hear about promises that came true so long ago?

 Think about it:
What do you think these promises mean for you?

 DO IT!
Take some time now to read about one of God's promises in the Bible. Draw a picture or write in your own words what that promise means to you.

What Hope?

For what hope does the
godless man have?
—*Job 27:8*

We're so lucky, you and I.

We have people who love us, who want us to know about God. We have people who take the time to tell us about God's promises to us. We have people around us who have been filled with the hope that only God gives, and it over-flows to you and to me.

But what about the people around *us*? Are we overflowing with the hope of God and letting them know where to find it too?

There are people out there who have never heard about God. They've never heard a whisper of the name of Jesus, never held a Bible in their hands.

Do you know anyone like that? Do your friends have the hope of God in their hearts? Does your cousin know that Jesus loves him? Find out! And when you do, let the hope in your heart overflow to them too.

 Tell me about it:

Name some people who share the hope of God with you.

 Think about it:

Who do you know who needs to hear about the love of Jesus?

 DO IT!

Draw a picture or write a special scripture, and give it to that person today.

Disappearing Hope

For many days neither sun nor stars appeared, and the severe storm kept raging. Finally all hope that we would be saved was disappearing.

—*Acts 27:20*

In the book of Acts, we read about Paul on a ship, sailing straight for trouble. He had warned the captain about the stormy seas ahead, but the captain ignored him, determined to reach an island where they would spend the winter.

Then the storm came. It drove the boat out into the ocean, beating it with rain and battering it with wind. The men threw out much of their cargo to lighten their load, but still the wooden boat creaked and crashed in the waves. Hope was disappearing fast.

But Paul's hope was in God. An angel had already told him that he and everyone aboard the ship would be safe, so Paul shared that hope with the others—all 275 of them. Before long, the people were shipwrecked, and the boat was splintered, but God's promise stood true. Not one life was lost. The stranded sailors swam to the nearest island, where they were welcomed and cared for by the people who lived there.

As the boat crumbled beneath Paul's feet, he held tight to the promises of God. And God's promises shone brightly, even through the darkest storm.

 Tell me about it:

Have you ever felt your hope disappear?

 Think about it:

What happened? What did you do?

 DO IT!

Draw a picture of Paul's ship in the storm. Show the light of God's hope shining through.

Hope in Justice

I hope in Your judgments.
—*Psalm 119:43*

Judgment may not seem like something you'd place your hope in, but let's think about it for a minute. What if there were none?

Sure, you'd love for Mom to just forget about that cookie you snuck before dinner. But what if that were true for everyone? What if no one ever received judgment? What if people were never punished when they did something wrong? Can you imagine what the world would be like?

So even though "judgment" isn't always fun, it *is* another reason we can put our hope in God. He sees every person and everything they do, right or wrong. And He uses His godly wisdom to reward the good and to set the wrongs right.

 Tell me about it:

Why do we have rules?

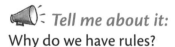

 Think about it:

Why do we get punished when we break those rules?

DO IT!

Make a list of five rules in your home. What does it look like when everyone follows those rules? What would it be like if everyone broke all of those rules?

Hope in Waiting

I wait for Yahweh; I wait and
put my hope in His word.
—*Psalm 130:5*

I remember waiting, as a child, for my daddy to get home from work. Every afternoon at four thirty, his old blue truck would rumble into the driveway, and I would burst out the front door and jump into his arms.

Every day I waited for my daddy. And every day I put my hope in his coming home. Even though I *knew* he was coming home, and I even knew what time, I still watched and waited with hope.

Let's watch and wait for the Lord in the same way. We can place our hopes in knowing that He's there, thinking about us and loving us. And we can watch and wait joyfully, with eyes wide open, just to see when He's going to show up next.

 Tell me about it:

Can you remember a time when you felt loved by God?

_____

_____

 Think about it:

How do you know that God is there, watching over you?

_____

_____

👋 *DO IT!*

Imagine God actually holding you in His arms. How would that feel? What would that look like? Draw a picture or write about it as you imagine it.

God's Chosen People

Israel, put your hope in the LORD,
both now and forever.

—*Psalm 131:3*

Israel was God's chosen people. In the Old Testament, we hear a lot about the Israelites, how they started with just one man and a promise from God. We see how they escaped from Egypt and an evil pharaoh. We watch God give them food and water in the wilderness and lead them into their promised land. Even after all the times that God provided for them and brought them to safety, Psalm 131:3 still reminds those people to put their hope in the Lord, "both now and forever."

See, that message wasn't just for God's chosen people thousands of years ago. That message is for God's chosen people of today and tomorrow. You and me. And generations to come.

Sometimes, even as God's people, even after all that He does to help us out, we need to be reminded where to look when we need hope. And that's okay. But we can know that without a doubt, He'll always be there helping us and guiding us, "both now and forever."

 Tell me about it:
Where do you think you'll be in five years? In fifty years?

 Think about it:
Where will God be in five years? In fifty years?

 DO IT!
Draw a picture of yourself in fifty years. What will you look like? What will you be doing?

Hope in Your Helper

Happy is the one whose help is
the God of Jacob, whose hope
is in the LORD his God.

—*Psalm 146:5*

When you're little, it seems you're always asking for help—with tying your shoes, reaching the cereal, doing your math. And sometimes you just can't wait until you're big enough to do it all on your own!

But do you want to know a secret from a grown-up? Even when you get big and *you're* the parent—tying shoes and reaching cereal and explaining math— you will *still* need help. Paying the bills and raising the kids and doing your job.

Lucky for us, big or little, parent or child, our Helper is always there. He may send His help in the form of a parent or a teacher or a good friend. But if we take our needs to Him, He will be faithful to help us. And as the psalmist reminds us, we are happy when our help and our hope comes from God.

You'll never get so big that you don't need the help of God.

 Tell me about it:

What are some things you still need help with?

_____

_____

_____

 Think about it:

What are some things you are now big enough to do on your own?

_____

_____

_____

 DO IT!

Talk to God about the things you need help with. And be happy that your help comes from Him.

Valuable You

The LORD values those who fear Him, those who put their hope in His faithful love.

—*Psalm 147:11*

Has anyone ever told you how much you're worth . . . how much God loves you and values you?

It can be hard to understand that the Creator of the entire universe, who made millions and billions of people, cares about little ol' you. But He does—it's true!

Luke 12:7 says that even "the hairs of your head are all counted." I would dare to guess that your parents don't even know how many hairs are on your head! But that's how much God knows about you, how much He cares about *you*.

The Creator of the universe has spoken: You are valued. You are loved. You are His.

 Tell me about it:

Why do you think you're important to God?

 Think about it:

What are some ways God shows us how much He values us?

 DO IT!

Go ahead. Just try to count the number of hairs on your head. Then thank God for loving you so much that He already knows.

Choose Wisely

Don't let your heart envy sinners; instead, always fear the LORD. For then you will have a future, and your hope will never fade.

—*Proverbs 23:17–18*

Sometimes life just doesn't seem fair. Sometimes it can seem like doing the right thing gets you nowhere. And sometimes it seems like the ones making trouble are the only ones having fun.

This isn't a new thing. It doesn't surprise God. And it shouldn't surprise us.

Thousands of years ago, when the wisest men were putting together the book of Proverbs, they wrote today's verse for you. God knew that one day you would have to make a choice.

When all of your friends are laughing at the new girl . . . When the mess in your room can all be hidden under the bed . . . When your brother is feeding his peas to the dog . . . Choose wisely. "For then you will have a future, and your hope will never fade."

 Tell me about it:

Have you ever seen someone do something wrong and get away with it? What happened?

 Think about it:

Why should you choose the right thing, even if no one will know?

DO IT!

Talk to God about making right choices. Ask Him to give you strength to follow in His ways.

Hope = Joy

The hope of the righteous is joy.
—*Proverbs 10:28*

Imagine a big pile of presents. Tall ones, skinny ones, great big boxy ones. Red stripes, yellow polka dots, and purple curly bows.

You immediately start thinking of all the things that could be inside. And you feel excited . . . happy . . . *hopeful.*

God has a big pile of surprises just waiting for your life. He's wrapping up things you've never even thought of. And by seeking His will and walking in His ways, you can hope, you can *know,* that one by one, you will unwrap those gifts for your life.

Expect great things from God, and that hope will bring you joy all the days of your life.

 Tell me about it:

What gifts has God already given you in your life?

 Think about it:

What kinds of gifts do you think He has waiting for you?

 DO IT!

Draw a picture of God's gifts. Include some of the gifts He's given you *and* some of the gifts you have yet to unwrap.

Stay Hopeful

Delayed hope makes the heart sick, but fulfilled desire is a tree of life.

—*Proverbs 13:12*

Staying hopeful can be hard! Worry will whine in your ear. Fear will creep into your mind. Waiting will seem to last forever.

But when fear and worry and waiting darken your day, remember to look for the ray of light shining through. That light is your hope, your reminder that God is in control and that He's working for your good.

Tell your fears that God controls them. Tell your worries that He will take care of you. And tell yourself that you can wait one more day (and another and another if you have to). When we choose to focus on the light, it can chase away the darkness every time.

 Tell me about it:

How do worry and fear affect our hopes?

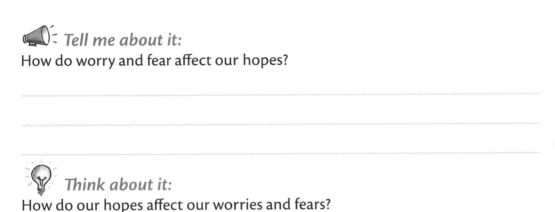

Think about it:

How do our hopes affect our worries and fears?

DO IT!

Get a flashlight and—carefully—go into a dark room. Turn on the flashlight and watch the light chase the darkness away.

You CAN

"Those who put their hope in Me
will not be put to shame."

—*Isaiah 49:23*

You are going to fail at some things in life.

There. I said it. And that's okay. Failing means that you tried. Failing will teach you what *not* to do. And failing will eventually teach you to do some things really, really well.

But whether you're winning or losing, there is no shame when your hope is in the Lord.

Philippians 4:13 reminds us, "I am able to do all things through Him who strengthens me." God will give us the strength to follow His path. And He will give us the strength to get back up when we fail. As long as our eyes are on Him and His grace, the world's idea of failure won't mean a thing.

Put your hope in Jesus. Trust Him. Follow Him. And you will be able to do anything He calls you to do.

 Tell me about it:

Describe a time when you failed at something.

 Think about it:

What did you learn from that failure?

 DO IT!

Write the words of Philippians 4:13 on a piece of paper. Use bright colors, decorate it with a fun border, and hang it where you and your family can see it.

Hope in Wisdom

If you find [wisdom], you will have a future, and your hope will never fade.

—*Proverbs 24:14*

Where is wisdom? Where would you look? Is it up in the sky? Or in a big book?

God gives us so many ways to learn about Him, to gain wisdom about our lives. Of course, the Bible, His Word, is the most complete source of wisdom He's given to us. But He has also surrounded us with people who love us and want to teach us about Him. Our parents and teachers and pastors can help us understand Bible stories and big words like *salvation* and *redemption*. Even just a walk outside, looking at a leaf or a feather or an ant, can tell you so much about this amazing world and the Creator who made it for you.

Be on the lookout for wisdom, wherever you go, and you will be sure to find it. And when you do, "you will have a future, and your hope will never fade."

 Tell me about it:

Where do you go to learn more about God?

_____

_____

Think about it:

What is one thing you've always wanted to know about God?

_____

_____

 *DO IT!*

Open your Bible or go to a parent or teacher and start looking for answers about that one thing.

Finding Strength

"You were tired out by the length of your road,
yet you did not say, 'It is hopeless.'
You found renewed strength,
therefore you did not faint."

—*Isaiah 57:10 NASB*

Imagine this: You're out shopping with Mom. It seems like you've walked down every single aisle of the store at least three times. Your little feet have to do double-time to keep up with her big steps. Your legs are Jell-O.

Do you . . .

      a) whine and complain, and scream, "It is hopeless!"?

      b) smile and find the strength to keep on going?

Read Isaiah 57:10 one more time. I think you know the answer. When life wears you down, look up and smile. You will find new strength in hope.

 Tell me about it:

When was the last time you just wanted to give up? What did you do?

_____

_____

_____

Think about it:

How can hope give us new strength?

_____

_____

_____

DO IT!

Memorize the words of Isaiah 40:31: "Those who trust in the LORD will renew their strength."

A Future and a Hope

"For I know the plans I have for you"—
this is the LORD's declaration—"plans
for your welfare, not for disaster, to
give you a future and a hope."
—*Jeremiah 29:11*

Just as God spoke the earth into being . . . just as He told the sun to shine . . . just as He declared the light "day" and the darkness "night". . . He has declared His plans for you.

It's hard to imagine, but before we were even born, God had plans for us. "We are His creation, created in Christ Jesus for good works, which God prepared ahead of time so that we should walk in them" (Ephesians 2:10). But to know what those plans are, we need to get to know God Himself. And as we grow closer to Him, we learn more about those plans He has for us.

Walk with Him, and He will lead you right to the plans He has for you.

 Tell me about it:

What do you want to be when you grow up?

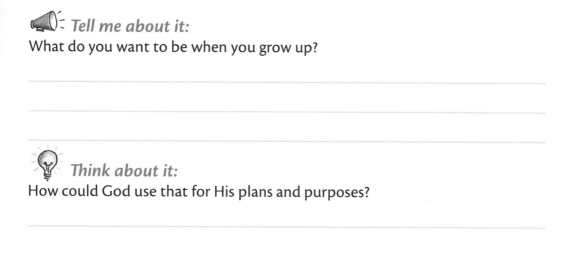 *Think about it:*

How could God use that for His plans and purposes?

🖐 *DO IT!*

Draw a picture of a grown-up you. Where will you be? What will you be doing?

Never-Ending Love

Yet I call this to mind,
and therefore I have hope:
Because of the LORD's faithful
love we do not perish,
for His mercies never end.

—*Lamentations 3:21–22*

No matter what you do, how old you get, how far you roam, God will always love you. His love is so big, so never-ending, that we as humans can't even imagine it.

In fact, 1 John 4:8 tells us that "God is love." So, as long as there is God—forever and ever!—there is love.

He loves you so much that "He gave His One and Only Son, so that everyone who believes in Him will not perish but have eternal life" (John 3:16). That, you can be sure, is a love like no other. And that, little one, is a love you can put your hope in.

 Tell me about it:

How much do you love your pet, your sister, or your parents?

_____

_____

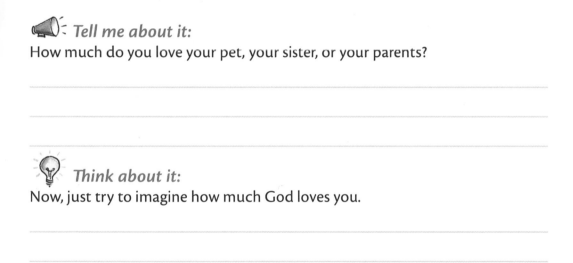 *Think about it:*

Now, just try to imagine how much God loves you.

_____

_____

_____

DO IT!

Draw a big heart, and write the words of John 3:16 in the center.

Get Rid of the Worries

Give all your worries to him, because he cares about you.

—*1 Peter 5:7* NCV

Do you know what the opposite of hope is? You guessed it: worry!

Hope is expecting something good to happen. Worry is thinking something bad will happen.

But the Bible tells us, "Don't worry about anything, but in everything, through prayer and petition with thanksgiving, let your requests be made known to God" (Philippians 4:6). I'll admit, that's a lot easier to read than to do. Still, with some practice, you can learn to skip all of the worrying and take it straight to God.

Hope can't grow the way it's supposed to when it's full of worry weeds. So the next time you feel your hope fading, make sure your worry isn't getting in the way. And if it is, well, get it out of there, and give it to God. He will take it from there.

 Tell me about it:

What are some hopes and some worries you have right now?

 Think about it:

How does it help to take our worries to God?

 DO IT!

Plant a seed, water it, and watch it grow. If any weeds pop up, toss them out immediately!

The Hope of the World

"The nations will put their hope in His name."
—*Matthew 12:21*

For thousands of years, the name of Jesus has brought hope to the world. The prophet Isaiah predicted it before Jesus was even born. And in Matthew 12:21, Jesus Himself points back to those words.

When Jesus spoke the words of Matthew 12:21, huge crowds were following Him. They had heard His teachings. They had seen His miracles. And they had put their hope in Him.

After Jesus went back to heaven, His followers continued His teachings. They told of His miracles and His love. They brought sinners to their Savior. And they placed their hope in Him.

Isaiah had predicted it. Jesus was seeing it happen then. And it is still happening today.

The One you put your hope in is a powerful Savior. He is everlasting. He has brought hope to the nations. And He will bring hope to you.

 Tell me about it:

Talk to a parent or a teacher about a time when our nation has come together and put its hope in the Lord.

 Think about it:

How does it help us as a nation when we put our hope in God?

 DO IT!

Find a token of our nation's hope in God. (Hint: look at that penny in your piggy bank.)

Hope Grows

But I will hope continually and will praise You more and more.

—*Psalm 71:14*

Wow! We have looked at *hope* in so many different ways. We've talked about how to find it and keep it. We've talked about the strength it can give us. We've talked about the *opposites* of hope: worry and hopelessness. And we've talked about how hope has shaped the lives of billions of people for thousands of years.

I *hope* by now this little word has become very real and very powerful for you. It's not just a word to be thrown around, as in, "I hope we have ice cream today." It's a powerful tool you can use. It is a force that will grow inside of you and brighten your days—if you will let it.

Keep thinking about it. Keep growing it. Keep *planting* it. You'll be amazed at how high hope grows.

 Tell me about it:

How has the idea of hope grown for you?

 *Think about it:*

What are some ways you can plant hope in the lives of others?

 DO IT!

Find one way, today, to plant hope in someone's life.

Always Hope

Maintain love and justice, and always put your hope in God.

—*Hosea 12:6*

After all that we've learned about hope, there's one thing that you must never, ever forget: *always hope.*

Those two words will get you through so much. When things seem their darkest ... when there seems like no way out ... when you're ready to give up ... always hope.

It will lift you through the valleys. It will carry you over the mountains. It will give you light when there is none to be found.

The Bible tells us that faith, hope, and love are the three things that will last forever (1 Corinthians 13:13). Whatever may come your way, it will not outlast hope or faith or love.

Hope always. "And always put your hope in God."

 Tell me about it:

When you're facing tough times in the future, describe what it will look like to "always put your hope in God."

 Think about it:

If you know that hope lasts forever, does this change the way you look at your future? How?

 DO IT!

Make a sign for your room with the words of Hosea 12:6: "Always put your hope in God."

Love

Love Is

This is how we know
what love is: Jesus Christ
laid down his life for us.
—1 John 3:16 NIV

We can't talk about love without talking about Jesus. He is the ultimate example of the most amazing love. God sent Him as a sacrifice for us. And when it was time, Jesus willingly, lovingly laid down His life in exchange for ours.

It doesn't even make sense—except that it is *love*.

Jesus is perfect, without sin. But He gave up His life to pay for ours. His sacrifice paid for the sins of the world. We could never understand it, and we will never live up to a love like that. But we can certainly spend the rest of our lives trying.

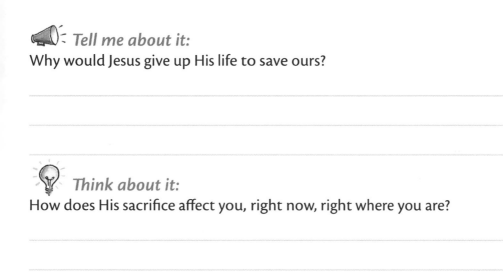

Tell me about it:

Why would Jesus give up His life to save ours?

 Think about it:

How does His sacrifice affect you, right now, right where you are?

DO IT!

Thank God right now for His sacrifice and love.

Patient and Kind

Love is patient, love is kind.
—*1 Corinthians 13:4*

Loving others isn't always easy. But if we want to love the way Jesus did, we need to look at how the Bible describes that love. Then we need to try our best to love in that way.

Here's one where we could *all* probably use a little work: love is *patient* and *kind*.

It's not that we lose our patience on purpose. Or that we *mean* to be unkind. Sometimes it just comes out. But this verse tells us that if we are acting in love, we are patient. And we are kind. Period.

Only Jesus can love with perfect patience and perfect kindness. But I know that if we try, we can all find a way to show a little more patience and kindness every day.

 Tell me about it:

What usually causes you to lose your patience? When is it hard to be kind?

 Think about it:

What does it look like to show love with patience and kindness? Give some examples.

 DO IT!

Find a small, flat rock. With a marker, write "patient" on one side and "kind" on the other. Carry it as a reminder to help you be patient and kind.

Love Is Not

Love does not envy, is not boastful, . . .
does not act improperly, is not selfish, is
not provoked, and does not keep a record
of wrongs.
—*1 Corinthians 13:4–5*

First Corinthians also tells us what love is *not*—a braggy, bratty, stingy, touchy tattletale.

We're all guilty. Sometimes we get a little too proud of ourselves. Sometimes it's tough to share. And sometimes, well, we've just had enough!

But if we're really trying to love people the way God wants us to, we should work toward the opposite of that list—humble, well-behaved, generous, easy-going, and forgiving.

Smile. Share. Give a little grace. And remember that you're doing it all in the name of love, God's way.

Tell me about it:

Which of those "nots" in 1 Corinthians 13:4–5 are you guilty of?

_____

_____

_____

Think about it:

How do you think those "nots" make God feel?

_____

_____

_____

DO IT!

Label one side of your paper "Do" and the other "Do Not." Under each, draw examples of how love does and does not look.

Why Love?

God is love, and the one who remains in love remains in God, and God remains in him.

—1 John 4:16

Why does it matter how we love? Or if we even show love at all?

The Bible tells us, "God is love." When we love, we look like Him. We make Him happy. And we point people toward Him.

Just as important, when we show love to others, we, too, grow closer to God. And God grows closer to us (James 4:8). When we love, we learn even more about love and how to love the right way. We learn more about God and His character. Because, after all, "God is love."

When you think about it that way, this love stuff is really important. Don't take it lightly. Show love in a big way today.

 Tell me about it:

"God is love." What exactly do you think that means?

_____

_____

🔦 *Think about it:*

How has God shown that He is a loving God?

_____

_____

✋ *DO IT!*

Draw a heart. In the center, write, "God is love. 1 John 4:16." Now color it, cut it out, and give it away.

Real Love

Your love must be real.
Hate what is evil, and hold
on to what is good.

—*Romans 12:9* NCV

What if you forget all these verses? What if you don't remember what God says about love? How can you know if you're showing love in the right way?

Well, Romans 12:9 makes it pretty simple. Get rid of the bad. Hold on to the good. Jealousy? Gone. Kindness? Keep it. Anger? Toss it. Helpfulness? YES. Love *that* way. That's how you know your love is real. Sincere. The way God wants us to love.

 Tell me about it:

What are some words that describe the way God wants us to love?

_____

_____

Think about it:

Think about the way you've treated others lately. What was good about it? What do you need to get rid of?

_____

_____

DO IT!

Make two lists: Good and Bad. List some bad behaviors you need to get rid of and some good ones to hold on to.

No Fear

There is no fear in love; instead,
perfect love drives out fear.

—1 John 4:18

Jesus loved with a fearless love. Evil spirits, skin diseases, and sinful pasts—nothing could scare Him away from healing and showing grace to others.

Jesus loved with a perfect love. He saw people through perfect eyes. Instead of being clouded with the fear of the world, Jesus saw others the way His heavenly Father saw them: wonderfully made children of God.

When you look at others, what do you see first? Their clothes? Their hair? Or their hearts?

With everyone you meet, try to look at them as if you're looking through the eyes of God, perfect eyes that see with a perfect love.

 Tell me about it:

What can make us fearful about loving others?

Think about it:

What are some ways we can overcome fear to love like Jesus does?

DO IT!

Write down something nice about someone you know.
Give him the note the next time you see him.

The Biggest Love

This is love: not that we loved God,
but that he loved us and sent his Son
as an atoning sacrifice for our sins.
—1 John 4:10 NIV

You can't out-love God. No matter what you do or how you grow in love, the fact will always remain: He loved you first. He sent a gift to you that you can't give back. He gave the ultimate sacrifice for love.

But that doesn't mean we should stop trying. That just means that every time we have trouble loving someone God's way, we can go to Him. It also means that every time we're feeling not so loved ourselves, we can go to Him.

God is the love expert. He *is* love. You can't out-love Him. And you can never escape the love He has for you.

 Tell me about it:

How would you describe God's love for you?

_____

_____

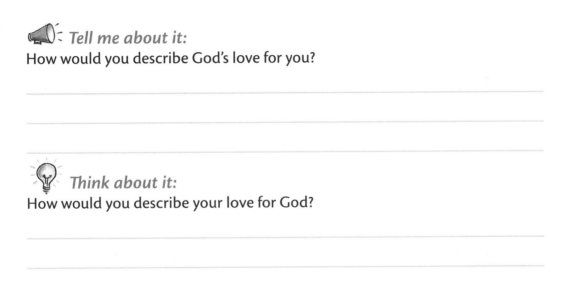 *Think about it:*

How would you describe your love for God?

_____

_____

DO IT!

Rewrite 1 John 4:10 in your own words.

In This Way

"For God loved the world in this way: He gave His One and Only Son, so that everyone who believes in Him will not perish but have eternal life."

—John 3:16

Do you know the words of John 3:16 by heart? It is one of the most well-known Bible verses. Parents and teachers ask kids to memorize this verse because it so perfectly and briefly explains God's love and sacrifice for the world.

In one sentence, John tells the whole salvation story: (1) God loved us, the sinners of this world. (2) He gave His Son to save us from sin. (3) Because of that sacrifice, we can have eternal life.

This is a verse that you want to keep in your heart forever. It will help you remember God's great love for you. And it will be a helpful tool in letting others know the sacrifice God made for them too.

 Tell me about it:

Why is it important for us to remember God's sacrifice for us?

_____

_____

_____

Think about it:

Why is it important for us to tell others about God's love for them?

_____

_____

_____

DO IT!

If you haven't already, memorize the words of John 3:16. Share it with someone who has never heard of God's love for him or her.

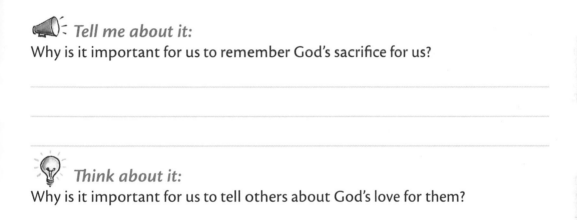

The Love of Christ

Who can separate us from the love of Christ?

—*Romans 8:35*

When the Scripture asks the question, "Who can separate us from the love of Christ?" . . . what is your answer?

Paul, the disciple who wrote Romans, asked this question. And then he answered it: "For I am persuaded that not even death or life, angels or rulers, things present or things to come, hostile powers, height or depth, or any other created thing will have the power to separate us from the love of God that is in Christ Jesus our Lord!" (Romans 8:38–39).

You see, Paul had been there. He had seen the face of death and lived. He had been at the mercy of rulers and "hostile powers." He had been shipwrecked and survived. He had been set free from prison chains by the miraculous love of Jesus.

When he answered his own question, he wasn't guessing. He wasn't imagining. He was talking about real life, his life, and how the love of Jesus grabbed him and never let him go.

Tell me about it:
How have you seen the love of Jesus in your life?

_____

_____

Think about it:
Try to think of the most powerful thing in the world. Could *that* separate you from the love of Christ?

_____

_____

DO IT!
Make your own list like Paul's: Not even _____ or _____ or _____ or _____ or _____ could separate me from the love of God in Christ Jesus!

The Palm of God's Hand

"Look, I have inscribed you on the palms of My hands."

—*Isaiah 49:16*

Whenever you're feeling small and unimportant, remember these words God spoke about His people: "I have you inscribed on the palms of My hands."

You are so important. The God of the universe thinks so much of you that your name is written on the palm of His hand. Hundreds of years after the prophet Isaiah recorded these words, Jesus would have nail-scarred hands that remind Him of the love He has for you.

Open up your own hands and take a close look. Wiggle your fingers. Drum your fingernails on the table. Look at the unique markings of your fingertips. Even in your own hands, you can see the work of God, who loves you and who made you perfectly unique.

 Tell me about it:

What do you think God is thinking about you right now?

_____

_____

 Think about it:

In what ways are you different from everyone else? In what ways are you the same?

_____

_____

 DO IT!

Using an inkpad or a washable marker, ink your fingertip and make a fingerprint on a piece of paper. Look at the perfect lines and designs that make you uniquely you.

You Are His Child

Look at how great a love the Father has given us that we should be called God's children.

—*1 John 3:1*

Have you ever won a million dollars? Had dinner with the president? Been given a free pass to an amusement park?

Maybe not. But you have something even better.

You know the owner of the universe? The almighty God? The Maker of heaven and earth? He has adopted you and called you *His*.

You have been given the greatest honor of being called a child of God. And with a status like that, what you do matters. How you treat others matters. How you love matters.

The world is watching. God has called you His. Now go and make Him proud.

 Tell me about it:

How is God like our earthly parents? How is He different?

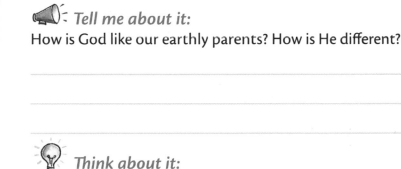 *Think about it:*

Looking back at your day, what was God proud of? What would He want you to do differently next time?

 *DO IT!*

Make a sign that says, "Child of God," and hang it on your mirror. Let it shape how you see yourself and how you see others.

Through Right and Wrong

Those whom I love, I reprove and discipline.

—*Revelation 3:19* NASB

When I was a kid, my mom would punish me and say, "This hurts me more than it hurts you." *Yeah, right,* I would think. *I'm the one being punished!*

But then I became the parent. And I have to say, discipline is absolutely no fun from this side either.

So why in the world would we do something that hurts us *both*? Well, because it doesn't really. In the long run, both parent and child benefit from good discipline. When your parents punish you for doing something wrong, even though it hurts, you learn not to do that thing again. And when you stop the bad behavior, everyone is better off as a result.

Besides, if God is love, and He disciplines us, then our parents must be on to something good.

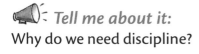 *Tell me about it:*

Why do we need discipline?

 Think about it:

Can you think of a time when you were actually glad that you got in trouble?

 DO IT!

Thank your parents for doing the tough job of disciplining. And while you're at it, thank God for it too.

Gracious Love

The LORD is compassionate and gracious, slow to anger and rich in faithful love.

—*Psalm 103:8*

I don't know about you, but I don't even want to count the number of times I mess up on a given day. Saying hurtful things, thinking selfish thoughts, and just not trying my very best—sometimes it all happens before I even realize it!

God knows we're not perfect. Adam and Eve proved that long, long ago in the garden of Eden. And we humans have been proving it every day since.

We can try each day to do better, to look more like Jesus, but in the meantime, we have Psalm 103:8. Our God who disciplines us is also "compassionate," "gracious," "slow to anger," and "rich in faithful love." His love will not abandon us when we mess up. In fact, His compassion may just step in and show us grace.

Our God is not an angry, hateful God. Our God is *love*.

 Tell me about it:

What is one way you messed up today?

_____

_____

 Think about it:

How can you avoid messing up in the same way tomorrow?

_____

_____

 DO IT!

On a piece of paper, write those four descriptions of God: *compassionate, gracious, slow to anger,* and *rich in faithful love.* Then beside each one, write an example of how you could love in that way today.

He Loved Us First

We love because He first loved us.

—1 John 4:19

Why do we love? It's not because we're nice people. It's not because other people deserve it. It's not even because God tells us to. It's because He first loved us.

God created us in His image of pure, perfect love. And He sets the example for us every time He loves us. He loves us because He created us. He loves us because we are His. He loves us when we don't deserve it, and even when we don't love Him back.

He loves us. He *loves* us. *He loves us.*

And because He does, we can love Him. We can love others. We can love ourselves.

Because He loved us first.

 Tell me about it:

When do you think God first started loving you?

 Think about it:

When did you start loving God?

 DO IT!

Think of someone who needs to know that God loved him first. Then find a way to tell him.

Where Is Love?

May the Lord direct your hearts to God's love and Christ's endurance.
—*2 Thessalonians 3:5*

Loving people is tough. They can be lazy, crazy, snippy, and just plain mean. Just like me. And you.

Don't you wish you could just stop and ask for directions sometimes? Which way is the *right* way to love these hardheaded people? How would Jesus deal with that kind of person right now?

Well, you can.

God is always there to "direct your heart" in the right way to love, the way of "God's love and Christ's endurance." God's love is pure and perfect. And Christ's endurance is everlasting.

When the path to loving people gets scary and overgrown, stop and ask for directions. God will lead the way.

 Tell me about it:

When was a time recently that you needed help in loving others?

 Think about it:

Where are some places you could look for directions?

 DO IT!

Think of one issue or question you've had lately in dealing with others. Go, right now, and look for God's answers to that question.

All Things for Good

We know that all things work together for the good of those who love God.
—*Romans 8:28*

Ever have those days when everything just seems to go wrong? Well, it seemed like Joseph was having one of those *lives*. Through dreams, God had told Joseph that he would be a great leader someday. But his big brothers would have none of that. Jealous and sneaky, they sold him to a group of traders and told their father that Joseph had been killed. The traders sold Joseph as a servant in Egypt. But God kept promoting Joseph until he was second to only the pharaoh himself.

Then the famine hit. And thanks to Joseph's godly wisdom, Pharaoh's kingdom was the only place around where you could find food. Meanwhile, back in Canaan, Joseph's brothers were out of food. And guess where they had to go to get it. Yep, to Joseph, the brother they had sold into slavery.

But Joseph saw it all as the work of God. He told his brothers, "You planned evil against me; God planned it for good" (Genesis 50:20). Then Joseph gave his brothers food and land, and they all lived together again.

So, when you're having one of those days—or even one of those *lives*—take it from Joseph: even when it doesn't seem like it, God is working. And He is working for your good.

 Tell me about it:
Think for a minute about some bad things that have happened.

 Think about it:
Now try to think of the good that has come from those things.

 DO IT!
Over the next week, read the story of Joseph in Genesis 37, 39–47. Think about all the ways that God was working for his good.

You Can't Even Imagine

What eye did not see and ear did not hear, and what never entered the human mind—God prepared this for those who love Him.

—*1 Corinthians 2:9*

God is not only working for our good—He is preparing wonderful things for us beyond our greatest imagination.

Go ahead. Try it. Think of the most amazing things God could ever do for you. Think of where you could be, what you could be doing, your surroundings, the people who are with you. Let your imagination run wild.

Yep. It's better than *that*. Beyond our greatest imagination.

Remember who you're dealing with here! This is the God who created crickets to make music with their legs. He made chameleons that could change their own skin color. He made kiwi and kumquats and dragon fruit. He has made fascinating creations that are long extinct and creatures we haven't even discovered yet.

So trust me when I tell you—when the Bible tells you—that you cannot even begin to imagine all the things God has planned for you. If you listen to Him and follow Him, you will see those plans come true. They won't be the same as your plans—they will be even better than you could imagine.

 Tell me about it:

Out of all God's creations, what is your favorite?

 Think about it:

What do you think He is creating for *you*?

 DO IT!

Just for fun, create something. Draw it. Mold it out of clay. Build it with Popsicle sticks and glue. Imagine the fun God is having while making plans for you.

How Do We Love God?

"The one who has My commands and keeps them is the one who loves Me."

—John 14:21

Kitten snuggles. Blue skies. Fresh-baked cookies. Mama's lullabies. We are surrounded by reminders of God's love every day. But how do we show God that we love Him back?

Jesus told His disciples simply, "If you love Me, you will keep My commands" (John 14:15). It's simple. But it isn't easy.

Every day, before your feet hit the floor, you have to decide to behave the way God wants you to. You have to choose to love everyone the way Jesus would. You have to remember that you are His hands and feet, sent out to do His work.

We have been given a love that we can never, ever repay. And all that He asks is that we keep His commands.

 Tell me about it:

What are some of God's commands?

 Think about it:

How can you follow those commands today?

 DO IT!

Thank God now for the love He has shown us, and ask for His strength and guidance in keeping His commands.

The Most Important Command

He said to him, "Love the Lord your God with all your heart, with all your soul, and with all your mind. This is the greatest and most important command."

—Matthew 22:37–38

Before we can keep God's commands, we need to know what they are. We can do this by reading our Bible and spending time with God each day.

However, one man in the Bible had the chance to ask Jesus about God's commands face-to-face. And by reading our Bible, we are able to hear the answer for ourselves. The man asked Jesus which of God's commands was the greatest. And Jesus replied with the words, "Love the Lord your God with all your heart, with all your soul, and with all your mind."

The man who had asked the question was an expert in the law. But Jesus didn't point the man to a list of rules. He pointed him to God. To *loving* God before anything else. And doesn't that make perfect sense? Because when we do that one, most important command, all the others just fall into place.

 Tell me about it:

Think about all the rules you know God wants us to follow.

 Think about it:

How does the greatest commandment cover all the other rules?

 DO IT!

Make a list of rules. Write, "#1: Love the Lord your God with all your heart, with all your soul, and with all your mind." The end. Follow that one rule today and every day.

Love Your Neighbor

"The second is like it:
Love your neighbor as
yourself."
—*Matthew 22:39*

Just after the greatest command—to love God with all your heart, soul, and mind—Jesus tells us the second. "Love your neighbor as yourself."

Most of us are pretty good at loving ourselves. We eat good food. We play and have fun. We buy cool stuff. And that's totally okay.

In fact, Jesus knew we would take good care of ourselves. That's why He told us to love our neighbors in that same way. Do you like chocolate chip cookies? Share some with your neighbor. Want to feel happy and loved? Smile at your neighbor. Want the best for your life? Want the best for your neighbor.

Everything you need to know about loving others, you've already got, there within yourself.

 Tell me about it:

What are some of your favorite things?

 Think about it:

How could those things be used to show love to others?

 DO IT!

Make a list of five people. Beside each person, write one thing you both enjoy. How could you use that thing to show love to that person?

Be an Example

"By this all people will know that you are My disciples, if you have love for one another."

—*John 13:35*

How do you know that a teacher is a teacher? An artist is an artist? A dad is a dad?

A teacher teaches. An artist creates art. And a dad, well, he *dads*.

God is love. Jesus is love. And how will people know we are His followers? By the way we love.

We don't have to be perfect. We don't have to wear a uniform. We don't have to speak a certain language. We just have to love.

When we love like Him, the world will know that we are His. And then maybe the world will learn to love like Him too.

 Tell me about it:

Based on your actions, who do people think you are?

_____

_____

Think about it:

What have you done this past week to show you are a disciple of Jesus?

_____

_____

DO IT!

Draw a large rectangle, separated into five equal panels (like a comic strip). In each panel, draw a different action that would show you are a disciple of Jesus.

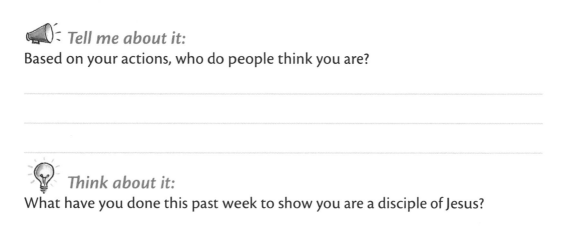

If . . .

Dear friends, if God loved us in this
way, we also must love one another.
—*1 John 4:11*

If the Creator of the universe hung the stars for us to see . . .
    If the one true God wonderfully made you and me . . .
If the Maker of heaven and earth gave all He had to give . . .
    If our God sent His only Son to die that we may live . . .
If He showed us all how to love our sister and brother,
    Then we, dear friends, we must love one another.

 Tell me about it:

What are some ways God loves us?

 Think about it:

Why does that mean we "must love one another"?

 DO IT!

Make a list of all the ways God loves you. Try to love others in just as many ways.

A Never-Ending Task

"This is My command: Love one another as I have loved you."
—*John 15:12*

The disciples had watched Jesus teaching and preaching tirelessly. They had seen Him do miracles and heal people on the spot. The woman no one wanted to talk to? Jesus sat with her at the well. The man with a skin disease? He touched him and made him clean. The outcasts, the sick, the sinners—Jesus loved them all.

But He wasn't finished yet. Soon He would carry an unbearably heavy cross to the top of a hill where He would be put on display for everyone to see. People would laugh at Him, mock Him, and call Him names while His friends wept at His feet. And even though He could call angels down to heal Him and rescue Him on the spot, He would stay. He would stay until His earthly life was gone. And we were paid for.

Our task of loving people is never done, sweet friend—not until we have loved as He loves.

 Tell me about it:
Why do you think Jesus asked us to love like He did?

 Think about it:
What are some ways that you can love like Jesus, right where you are?

DO IT!
Thank Jesus right now for the love He has shown us. Ask Him to help you love as He loves.

Everything in Love

Your every action must be done
with love.

—*1 Corinthians 16:14*

Okay, now. This is where it gets tricky. Sure, every once in a while, you can take cookies to your neighbor. Or say hi to the new kid. But *every* action? Uh-oh.

When I'm sweeping the kitchen? Love. *When I'm walking the dog?* Love. *When I'm listening to a dad speech?* You got it. Love.

When we think about loving others, we usually only think about the ways we love others *on purpose*. But God challenges us to show love in every. single. thing. we. do.

Why? Maybe because He knows that our on-purpose love doesn't mean a thing if everything else is grumpy. Those cookies take on a whole new sweetness when the neighbor sees you walking the dog with a smile. And after you say hi to the new kid, he keeps watching to see how you treat everyone else.

The every-now-and-then acts of love are great. But don't stop there. *Live* it. Live a life of love.

 Tell me about it:

Look back at your week. What are some ways you have loved others on purpose?

_____

_____

Think about it:

What are some ways you've loved others without realizing it?

_____

_____

 DO IT!

Try it today. Let your *every action* be done in love.

Love Your Enemies

"But I tell you, love your enemies and pray for those who persecute you."
—*Matthew 5:44*

What is your first reaction when someone makes you mad? What do you say to that kid who is always picking on you? Or when your brother breaks another one of your toys?

I'm guessing your first reaction is probably not love. If it were, Jesus wouldn't have to tell us, "Love your enemies . . . Pray for those who persecute you."

But Jesus knew we'd have troubles, and He knew we would need help in reacting to those troubles. He told His disciples, "You will have suffering in this world. Be courageous! I have conquered the world" (John 16:33).

He knew that people would pick on us, laugh at us, and make fun of us because He had already been there. And He knew how to make it through.

He loved His enemies and prayed for those who persecuted Him. He asks that we do too.

 Tell me about it:
In the past, how have you treated those who made you mad or picked on you?

_____

_____

_____

Think about it:
Did that help the situation? Or not? How?

_____

_____

DO IT!
Say a prayer for those who came to mind just now. Ask God for guidance in dealing with them.

Do Love

The commandments: Do not commit adultery; do not murder; do not steal; do not covet; and whatever other commandment—all are summed up by this: Love your neighbor as yourself.

—*Romans 13:9*

Some people think the Bible is a big, scary book full of don'ts. Yes, it has some don'ts to keep us safe and healthy. But it also has some DOs. And there is a whole lot of "Hey, look what God did!" and "Wow, He loves you!" Overall, the Bible is the story of how God loves His people—and the story of how we should love one another.

It's a story that started in Genesis and is still going on today. And only *we* can decide what part we play. We can be the story that says, "Hey, don't do what *that* guy did!" Or the one that reads, "Wow, let's all be like him."

As 1 John 3:11 tells us, "This is the message you have heard from the beginning: We should love one another." So, together, let's choose to keep writing this everlasting story of love.

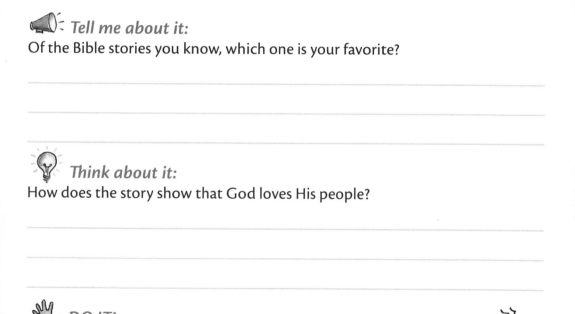

Tell me about it:
Of the Bible stories you know, which one is your favorite?

_____

_____

_____

Think about it:
How does the story show that God loves His people?

_____

_____

_____

DO IT!
Draw a scene from your favorite Bible story about God's great love for us.

Love Changes the World

Above all, maintain an intense love for each other, since love covers a multitude of sins.

—1 Peter 4:8

Just think of how much different the world would look if everyone followed 1 Peter 4:8!

Maybe you can't change the behavior of everyone in the world. But you can most certainly better the world by changing your own. If you "maintain an intense love" in everything you do, you can be sure that love and kindness will spread and grow, quite literally making the world a better place.

Let's say that you open the door for a lady at the store, and she walks in with a smile. The cashier sees her and smiles back. The smiling cashier reminds the man buying groceries to take some soup to his brother. The sick brother gets warm soup and a caring visitor. And they all feel happy and loved because you opened the door for the lady at the store!

You never know what impact your actions will have. But know this: you can change the whole world with a little bit of love.

 Tell me about it:

What is one act of love that you have done lately?

 Think about it:

Who else could have been affected by that one act?

 DO IT!

Draw a circle graph of your one action. Start by writing what you did in the middle and draw a circle around it. Then draw lines from it to other circles with other people who could have been affected or other actions started by your one action. See how big the graph can grow!

The Opposite of Love

Hatred stirs up conflicts, but love covers all offenses.
—*Proverbs 10:12*

The opposite of love, of course, is *hate*. It's a word I don't even like to say. Is there anything that deserves the *opposite* of love? Even Brussels sprouts should get a chance!

Psalm 97:10 tells us one thing we should hate: "You who love the LORD, hate evil!" When we love God, learn about Him, and try to follow in His ways, we usually know evil when we see it. It may not be in a red costume with horns, but something just tells us to run, not walk, in the other direction. And we should. But only then is hate a healthy thing to do.

When we show hate toward others—and even toward Brussels sprouts!—it doesn't make anything better. It just stirs up more conflict, causing trouble for everyone involved.

 Tell me about it:

When did you show hate when you should have shown love?

 Think about it:

Why would hateful actions stir up conflict?

 DO IT!

Write a note to truly apologize for a time when you acted hatefully. By doing so, you'll show love, a love that "covers all offenses."

Love in Tough Times

A friend loves at all times, and a
brother is born for a difficult time.

—*Proverbs 17:17*

Climbing trees and chasing butterflies. Riding bikes and flying kites. Having friends to play with is truly a gift from God.

But friends are also important—maybe the *most* important—during times when things aren't so fun. When you're sick or sad or just plain mad, there is nothing like a good friend to brighten your day.

Sometimes our friends can be having a bad day and we'll never even know it. They may not want to talk about a sick grandmother or the trouble they're having at home. This is why good friends love "at all times." We just never know when our friends may need us most.

 Tell me about it:

Who are some of your best friends right now?

 Think about it:

What are your favorite things about them?

 *DO IT!*

Write funny notes or draw pictures for your friends, just to make them smile.

Love in Action

Little children, we must not love
with word or speech, but with
truth and action.

—*1 John 3:18*

Have you ever just sat and watched an army of ants? One ant by himself doesn't seem to do much, but *together*? When you look at the whole group, they're digging tunnels and building dirt mounds and bringing home food ten times their size!

God has written the book on love. He showed us the ultimate sacrifice of love. Then He created us and sent us out, like an army of little love ants, into the world. One single person may not seem to be doing much. But when we work together and listen to the One in charge, we're moving mountains. We are changing the world.

Be a little love ant today. Put your love in action, and just watch those mountains move!

 Tell me about it:

How does working together make us stronger?

 Think about it:

Just imagine how many people are on this earth, working for God. Imagine what we could do if we all worked together.

 DO IT!

Draw a bunch of colored hearts. In the center of each one, write a different act of love.

Without Love

If I have the gift of prophecy and understand all mysteries and all knowledge, and if I have all faith so that I can move mountains but do not have love, I am nothing.

—*1 Corinthians 13:2*

I can be the smartest girl in the room, have all the latest gadgets, wear the coolest clothes, have perfect posture, shiny hair, and a sparkling smile. But without love, "I am nothing."

We live in a world that seems to want all the cool people and all the shiny stuff. And it's easy to get distracted by that. After all, "man sees what is visible, but the LORD sees the heart" (1 Samuel 16:7). But the reason I am writing this book—the reason you are reading it—is that God wants us to remember the real reason we are here: to spread His Word and His love to the ends of the earth.

When we love others the way God wants us to, He sees us as the coolest people in the room. And really, is there anything that matters more than that?

 Tell me about it:

What do you like most about yourself?

 Think about it:

What do you think God likes most about you?

 DO IT!

Pretend to be a newscaster. Share the breaking news of 1 Corinthians 13:2!

Show Big Love

Let no one despise your youth; instead, you should be an example to the believers in speech, in conduct, in love, in faith, in purity.

—*1 Timothy 4:12*

Don't ever think—not for a single second—that because you are little, you can't show big love. Little ones have the brightest eyes and the sweetest smiles. Little ones love bigger than anyone I know. Your little acts of love can make a bigger impact than anyone in the world.

I know for a fact that a little hug for your mama can change her entire day. A note to your daddy will keep him smiling no matter what else piles up on his desk. And a kind word to your teacher helps make her job worthwhile.

More than anything, with every act of love, you are an example to all those around you. Those younger than you are looking up to you. Those older than you are changed by your kindness. And you, too, grow a little bigger inside every time you love.

 Tell me about it:
Who around you is watching what you do and how you love?

 Think about it:
How have you already changed your world with little acts of love?

 DO IT!
Look in the newspaper, library, or online for young people your age who have made a big difference by loving others. Think about how you could do the same.

Gongs and Cymbals

If I speak human or angelic languages but do not have love, I am a sounding gong or a clanging cymbal.

—*1 Corinthians 13:1*

When playing along with a band, the cymbal sounds great, adding a big *oomph* right when the music needs it. But by itself, well, the cymbal doesn't really make music. It doesn't even sound nice. The cymbal is just plain loud. And kind of annoying. (Sorry, cymbal.)

First Corinthians warns us about being clanging cymbals. When we talk about God and the Bible, whenever we speak at all, we need to say things in love. Or else we're only being noisy.

Let's make some beautiful music today by saying and doing everything in love.

 Tell me about it:

What is one message that you feel is important, that you would like to share with someone?

_____

_____

Think about it:

Who would you share it with?

_____

_____

DO IT!

Share that message quietly today, in love.

Faith, Hope, Love

Now these three remain: faith, hope, and love. But the greatest of these is love.

—*1 Corinthians 13:13*

One hundred different days, in a hundred different ways, we have talked about faith, hope, and love. I hope you've grown deeper in your faith, set your hopes high, and learned how to show big love. But more than that, I want you to know: the journey does not end here.

These three things—faith, hope, and love—they last forever. From here to eternity, your faith will carry you, your hope will drive you, and your love will guide you. Nurture them and use them wisely.

Put your faith in God. Hang your hopes on Him. And remember that He is love.

 Tell me about it:
Since we started this journey, how has your faith grown?

 Think about it:
How have your hopes grown even higher?

 DO IT!
Draw a picture or write about how faith, hope, and love all work together to help us in this world and beyond.

THINKING SPACE

Use this space to complete your "Do It!" activities, and write down any other thoughts, questions, or doodles you have along the way.

221

Remember:

Now these three remain: faith, hope, and love. But the greatest of these is love.—1 Corinthians 13:13

Read:

In Luke 8:42–48, you can read a story about a sick woman who hoped that Jesus could make her well. She had such faith in His power; when she saw Him in a crowd, she believed that if she just touched the hem of His robe, she would be healed. And she was right! Jesus turned to her and said with great love, "Your faith has made you well. Go in peace." Do you see the examples of faith, hope, and love in this story? God knows how important those three principles are, and He wants them to be a big part of how we live our lives for Him!

Think:

1. Let's imagine. What would the world be like if faith, hope, and love didn't exist? What would it be like if everyone in the world had twice the faith, hope, and love they have now?

2. How far do you think faith can reach? Can you think of a way faith can help you even when life gets tough?

3. How high do you think hope can go? Do you have more hope than you did when you started this devotional?

4. How big is love? When is the last time you showed big love?

5. Think about Jesus' life. Can you name a time that He was faithful or hopeful? What about loving?